Awesome Asian Animals

A+
books®

Camels
Are
Awesome!

by Allan Morey

Consultant: Jackie Gai, DVM
Wildlife Vet

raintree
a Capstone company — publishers for children

Raintree is an imprint of Capstone Global Library Limited, a company incorporated in England and Wales
having its registered office at 7 Pilgrim Street, London, EC4V 6LB – Registered company number: 6695582

www.raintree.co.uk
myorders@raintree.co.uk

Edited by Michelle Hasselius
Designed by Peggie Carley
Picture research by Tracy Cummins
Production by Morgan Walters
Printed and bound in China.

ISBN 978-1-474-70250-8
19 18 17 16 15
10 9 8 7 6 5 4 3 2 1

British Library Cataloguing in Publication Data
A full catalogue record for this book is available from the British Library.

Acknowledgements
Alamy: Vic Pigula, 23; AP Images: Press Association, 22; Capstone Press: 11; Corbis: Tuul & Bruno Morandi,
25; iStockphoto: 49pauly, 19, Mordolff, 24; Shutterstock: aleksandr hunta, 11 Top, 14, Barbara Barbour, 7, Basti
Hansen, 10, Be Good, Cover Back, 1, 6, 30, David Aleksandrowicz, 16, eAlisa, 8 Top, Eric Isselee, Cover Middle
Left, Cover Top, Gustav, 13, 32, happystock, 28, John Carnemolla, 17, Jorge Felix Costa, 27, Mariia Savoskula,
12 Left, 4, 5, 20, murengstockphoto, 12 Right, 15, Nurlan Kalchinov, 8 Bottom, photowind, 18 Top, Rigamondis,
Design Element, smeola, Cover Bottom, Stephen Meese, 18 Bottom, Wolfgang Zwanzger, 9, Zazaa Mongolia, 29;
SuperStock: biosphoto, 21; Thinkstock: DanielPrudek, 26

We would like to thank Jackie Gai, DVM, for her invaluable help in the preparation of this book.

Every effort has been made to contact copyright holders of material reproduced in this book. Any omissions
will be rectified in subsequent printings if notice is given to the publisher.

All the internet addresses (URLs) given in this book were valid at the time of going to press. However, due to
the dynamic nature of the internet, some addresses may have changed, or sites may have changed or ceased
to exist since publication. While the author and publisher regret any inconvenience this may cause readers,
no responsibility for any such changes can be accepted by either the author or the publisher.

Contents

Amazing camels

Camels are known for the humps on their backs. But did you know a camel's hump is just a lump of fat? The fat helps camels to travel long distances without eating. A camel's hump is just one feature that makes this animal amazing.

A camel's hump acts as a snack that it carries on its back. The hump stores fat, which can be turned into energy. When a camel's hump looks large and plump, it is full. The camel is well fed.

When a camel's hump is small or flat, it doesn't have much fat. The camel needs more food and water.

One hump or two?

There are two types of camels. You can tell them apart by looking at their humps. Dromedary camels have one hump. Bactrian camels have two humps.

dromedary camel

Bactrian camel

Camels have small heads for their size. They also have long legs and necks. Camels look a bit like alpacas and llamas. That's because they are part of the same animal group.

For thousands of years, people have used camels to cross deserts. Millions of dromedary camels live in north Africa and the Arabian Peninsula. Most camels are tame. But small herds of wild Bactrian camels roam the Gobi Desert in Asia.

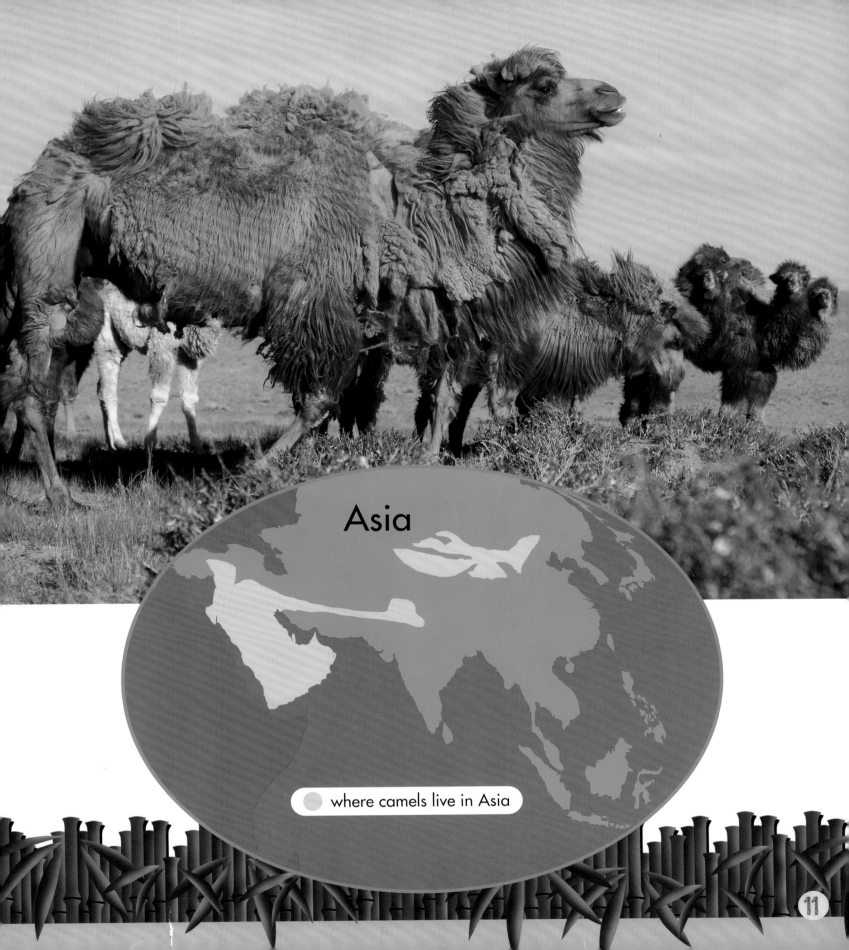

Asia

where camels live in Asia

Life in the desert

Camels have features that help them to live in hot, sandy deserts. Thick eyelashes shade their eyes from the blazing sun. They can close their nostrils to keep out sand.

Wink! You have two eyelids. A camel has three eyelids. A camel's extra eyelid blinks sideways to protect its eyes from sand.

Deserts can be very hot during the day. But they can be cold at night. **Brrrrr!** Bactrian camels have thick, woolly coats to keep them warm.

When a camel takes a step, its toes spread out. Skin between its toes stops the camel's feet from sinking into the soft sand.

A tough bite

Camels are herbivores. They eat plants. But most desert plants have sharp spines and pointy thorns. **Ouch!**

Luckily, a camel's upper lip is split.
A camel can move each part of its lip
separately. Camels use their upper
lips like fingers to grab prickly food.

Bulls, cows and calves

An adult male camel is called a bull. In the middle of winter, bulls start to get noisy. And stinky, too! They grunt and roar. They even foam at the mouth.

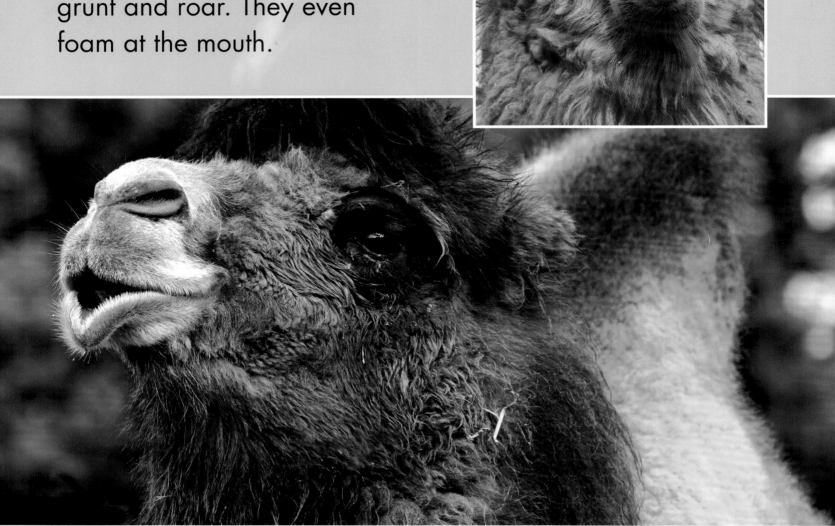

Bulls get smelly and act tough to attract mates. Female camels are called cows. After mating, the bull wanders off to be with other males. The pregnant cows gather together.

A pregnant cow gives birth to a calf 13 to 15 months after mating. Females usually have one calf at a time.

A newborn calf is about the size of a large dog. Less than an hour after birth, it can stand, walk and even run.

Calves don't have humps. Humps grow when calves start to eat plants instead of their mother's milk. Calves stay with their mothers for about two years.

Big desert animals

Many desert animals, such as snakes and lizards, are small. They cannot harm a camel. Adult camels are even too big for mighty lions to easily kill. A pack of wolves may chase down a wild camel. But most predators just leave camels alone. Healthy camels can live for up to 50 years.

Humans are the biggest danger to wild camels. People pollute places where camels live. They let goats graze in places where camels search for food. Some people kill camels for their meat.

Fewer than 1,000 Bactrian camels live in the wild. One day these camels could become extinct.

Camels are awesome

Today, some people in Asia race camels. Camels can run up to 64 kilometres (40 miles) per hour. That's as fast as a horse!

Camels are awesome. They can survive in harsh deserts. And people could never have crossed dry, sandy deserts without them.

Glossary

Bactrian type of camel that has two humps

dromedary type of camel that has one hump

energy strength to do activities without getting tired

extinct no longer living; an extinct animal is one that has died out, with no more of its kind

graze eat grass and other plants

herbivore animal that eats only plants

mate join together to produce young

pollute make something dirty or unsafe

predator animal that hunts other animals for food

pregnant carrying unborn young within the body; a pregnant female camel has one calf at a time

tame trained to live with or be useful to people

Books

Animals in Danger in Asia, Richard and Louise Spilsbury (Raintree, 2013)

Bactrian Camel (A Day in the Life: Desert Animals), Anita Ganeri (Raintree, 2012)

First Encyclopedia of Animals (Usborne First Encyclopedias), Paul Dowswell (Usborne Publishing Ltd, 2011)

Websites

www.bbc.co.uk/nature/life/Camel/
Learn interesting facts about camels.

http://gowild.wwf.org.uk/asia
Find out fun facts about camels, read stories and play games!

www.dudleyzoo.org.uk/our-animals/bactrian-camel
Learn about camels at the Dudley Zoological Gardens.

Comprehension questions

1. Look at the photo on page 6. Is this a dromedary or Bactrian camel? How do you know?

2. How does a camel's hump help it to travel long distances?

3. One day Bactrian camels may become extinct. What does "extinct" mean?

Index